Join Me for Tea

EMILIE BARNES
WITH ANNE CHRISTIAN BUCHANAN

Paintings by SUSAN RIOS

HARVEST HOUSE PUBLISHERS

Eugene, Oregon

Join Me for Tea

Text Copyright © 2002 by Emilie Barnes and Anne Christian Buchanan
Published by Harvest House Publishers
Eugene, Oregon 97402

ISBN 0-7369-0668-1

For more information about other books and products available from Emilie
Barnes, please send a self-addressed, stamped envelope to:

> More Hours in My Day
> 2150 Whitestone Drive
> Riverside, CA 92506
> (909) 369-4093

Original artwork © Susan Rios. Licensed by Art Impressions, Canoga Park, CA.
For more information regarding artwork featured in this book, please contact:

> Art Impressions
> 9035-A Eaton Avenue
> Canoga Park, CA 91304-1616
> (818) 700-8541

Text in this book previously appeared in *The Twelve Teas of Friendship*
by Emilie Barnes (Harvest House Publishers, 2001).

Design and production by Garborg Design Works, Minneapolis, Minnesota

Printed in Hong Kong.

02 03 04 05 06 07 08 09 10 11 /NG/ 10 9 8 7 6 5 4 3 2 1

CONTENTS

A Cup of Tea with Friends

*W*elcome to the wonderful world of tea and friendship. I have fondly selected a few of my favorite tea party ideas, delicious recipes, and simple craft projects from my latest book *The Twelve Teas of Friendship* to share with you. May your efforts to make new friends and cherish your old ones be richly blessed.

Through all the seasons of life, through the years, it's your friends who carry you through. What would you do without them—these chosen sisters who laugh with you, cry with you, and speak truth to you? And what better way to celebrate the warmth and intimacy of beautiful friendship than with the warmest and most intimate of celebrations—a tea.

That's the reason for this book. It's a collection of celebrations for you to share with friends you love—new friends and old, fun friends and friends in need, big groups of friends, and family friends. It's a book to help you celebrate—in your heart and in your home—the special friends who love and support you, who teach you and learn from you, who bring a special brightness to your good years and literally save you in your tough times.

What do you do with these friends at a tea party?

Well, for starters, you drink tea. But anyone who has enjoyed a childhood tea party knows you can hold a lovely tea without the tea. Fruit juice, hot chocolate, or even warm milk will serve just as well. You can even hold a tea party with iced tea.

There's food, of course. A well-appointed tea table might feature luscious warm scones with clotted cream, or elegant puff pastry with caviar, or even, in the case of the traditional British high tea, a full meal. However varied the fare, there's something about a warm cup of tea that brings out the best of savory or sweet.

You can also enjoy entertainment at your teas. Music at tea is traditional, whether it comes from a CD player in the background or a string quartet hired for the occasion. And you'd be very much in the teatime tradition to enjoy a small homegrown entertainment together afterward—a song around the piano, a short story read aloud, or even a mutually loved "chick flick."

There's so much you can do to enhance your enjoyment of the special times you spend with friends new and old. But don't think you have to fill every minute with activities. What you're there for is each other. You're there to talk and to listen and to enjoy the relationship-enhancing ritual of gathering around a beautiful table, of pouring tea for each other, of sharing delicious food, of being both formal and warm with one another.

In other words, *Join Me for Tea* is as much about friendship as it is about tea. Although it's full of easy recipes and fun ideas, its primary intention is to remind you just how precious your friendships are and how important it is to nurture them in a variety of ways—including the sharing of tea.

Emilie

A Gold-and-Silver Tea

Make new friends and keep the old,
One is silver and the other gold.

A fun and delicious way to meet new friends is to host a "share your friends" tea. Planned around a theme of silver and gold—for new friends and old—it's the kind of celebration that's guaranteed to brighten anyone's day.

This idea works best if you invite a group of women you know casually but not intimately. They can be coworkers, the mothers of your children's friends, people you've met at church, the spouses of your husband's colleagues—anyone you would enjoy getting to know better. But the fun really starts when you ask each guest to bring *another* friend—preferably someone you don't know. If you invite six people, you'll have a party full of twelve potential friends. To make the whole thing even more fun, ask one of your closest friends to host the party with you.

Although tea parties don't always require invitations, this is an occasion where an invitation can be very helpful. These can be as formal or informal as you like, as long as you explain the concept clearly and include your phone number so you'll know who is going to attend. The invitations will be extra special if you write or print them in gold or silver ink.

Name tags are also optional for a tea but especially helpful for this "get to know you" party. Here's a novel twist on the name tag idea that can serve as an icebreaker and help with your décor: Simply gather an assortment of small, inexpensive, gold and silver photo frames from your local closeout store. As each guest arrives, snap her picture with a Polaroid or a digital camera, write her name below her face with a permanent marker, and pop the photo in a frame. Arrange the photos on a sideboard or your tea table and urge the guests to use them as a reference for matching names and faces.

Teatime Treats

Menu Suggestions:

PERFECT POT OF TEA
SPICED HONEY STARS WITH ROYAL ICING
FRESH FRUIT ON SKEWERS
POUND CAKE WITH WHIPPED TOPPING

A PERFECT POT OF TEA

Although friends and fellowship are the central purpose for any tea party—and this one in particular—the star performer on any tea table is the tea itself. Here are a few tips on brewing a truly delightful six- to eight-cup pot of tea.

Good-quality loose tea (use 1 teaspoon of loose tea
    per cup plus one spoonful "for the pot") or tea bags
    (1 bag less than the number of cups you desire)
Boiling water
Milk, sugar, honey, or lemon, as desired

Begin by filling a teakettle with freshly
drawn cold water and putting it on to
boil. While the kettle is heating,
pour hot water into a ceramic or
glass teapot to warm it. (Brewing tea
in metal pots may impart a metallic
taste. It's fine, however, to transfer
the tea to a metal container once
it's brewed.) When the pot
has had time to warm, pour
out the hot water and add
the tea, then put the lid
back on the pot until
the water boils. As
soon as the kettle comes to
a rolling boil, remove from heat—don't over
boil. Pour boiling water into the teapot and let the tea
brew from three to six minutes. Lengthening the brewing
time will just make the tea taste bitter—if you want
stronger tea, use more tea leaves, not more time.

Gently stir the tea before pouring it through a tea
strainer into the teacups. (If you used tea bags, remove
them.) Serve with cream (really milk), sugar, honey, or
lemon. If your guests take milk, pour it into the cup first,
then add the tea.

SPICED HONEY STARS

These delicious little cookies are daintily spiced with a hint of orange. This recipe makes about 5 dozen cookies.

> ½ cup butter, softened
> ¾ cup sugar
> 1 egg
> ¼ cup honey
> grated peel of one small orange
> 2 cups flour
> 1 teaspoon baking soda
> 1 teaspoon cinnamon
> ½ teaspoon ground ginger
> ¼ teaspoon ground cloves
> Royal Icing (recipe below) and silver
>   baking ornaments

Preheat oven to 375°. Cream butter and sugar together thoroughly, then add eggs, honey, and orange peel and beat until smooth. Sift together flour, soda, and spices, then stir into butter mixture. Turn dough out onto well-floured surface (dough will be soft) and roll to ⅛-inch thickness. Cut out cookies with a 2-inch star-shaped cutter. Bake on ungreased cookie sheet for 7-8 minutes. Let stand for a few minutes before removing to wire racks to cool. Decorate as desired with Royal Icing and little silver candies.

ROYAL ICING

> 2 teaspoons powdered egg whites (meringue powder)
> 2 ⅔ cups confectioners' sugar
> ¼ cup water

Combine all ingredients and beat with electric mixer for 8-10 minutes, until peaks form and icing is the texture of sour cream. Thin icing with water a drop at a time until about consistency of honey. For each star, place a dollop of icing in the center and use a knife tip or chopstick to push the thin icing into a star shape on top of the cookie, leaving edges brown. Let icing harden before serving or storing cookies.

Crafter's Corner
A Gracious Invitation

Here's an easy and elegant homemade invitation that can adapt itself to a number of occasions. For each invitation, you'll need a heavy sheet of 8 ½ x 11-inch paper. You'll also need a pencil, scissors or a craft knife, gold and silver paint pens with a medium or wide point, a fine-point pen in blue or black, and a small piece of cardboard to make a template. If you want to mail the invitations, you'll need to purchase envelopes large enough to hold a 4 ¼ x 5 ½ -inch card.

To make the invitation, fold the sheet of paper in half, bringing the short edges together, then fold in half again. You should now have a folded 4 ¼ x 5 ½ -inch card.

Position it so that it opens like a book in front of you—with open edges at right and bottom. Mark the front or top surface of the card very lightly with a pencil. Open up the paper, which is now marked by the folds into rectangles, and look for the rectangle you

Make new friends

and keep the old,

One is silver and

the other gold.

—Old Rhyme

marked. Trace a 4-inch oval onto a piece of cardboard, cut it out to make a template, then center it on the front rectangle and trace around it. Carefully cut out this oval with scissors or a craft knife, then refold the card so that the front has an oval "window." With a pencil, lightly trace around the window onto the next layer of paper. Then use the silver and gold paint pens to draw a wavy "picture frame" around the oval, alternating scalloped silver and gold lines until the "frame" is about ½-inch thick. Outline the frame with the blue or black fine-tip pen and draw in alternating silver and gold lines behind the frame to suggest striped wallpaper. If you wish, add lines at top to suggest an old-fashioned wire picture hanger.

Open the card once more and find the oval you penciled in. Place the cardboard template over it, matching the edges to the penciled lines, and trace around the template with a black or blue fine-point pen. Use the same pen to write the little "silver and gold" poem found at the beginning of this chapter. When you refold the card once more, the poem should appear in the frame. Then open the card like a book and write your actual invitation inside.

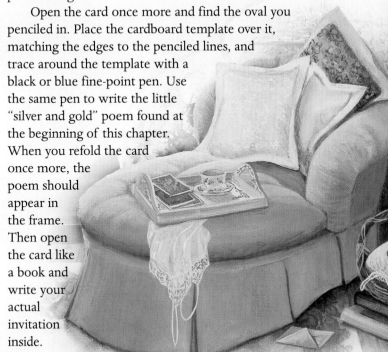

A "Just for Us" Tea

> *"Friendship," said Christopher Robin,*
> *"is a very comforting sort of thing to have."*
> —A. A. MILNE

Celebrate that special coziness between close friends by inviting two or three of your nearest and dearest for a snuggly teatime. Invite them on a Saturday morning for a teatime brunch—maybe after a "just us girls" sleepover—or on a blustery Sunday afternoon.

You don't need to restrict yourself to the dining room or living room for this special cozy tea. Seek out the most comfortable room in the house—the kitchen, the family room, a light-filled sunroom—even your bedroom. For a really creative twist, serve tea on bed trays on a big pillow-filled bed.

Ask everyone to wear their comfiest clothes—even robes and jammies. This isn't a formal, good-manners tea, though of course you always want to treat your friends with special courtesy. Concentrate on warmth and comfort—and make sure your special guests know they can stay as long as they like; they're part of the family. You might even want to greet each guest at the door with a new pair of deliciously warm bedroom slippers—or bring them into the kitchen to help you cook. (There's more time to talk if you're making the goodies together!)

This is the perfect kind of tea to precede or follow an indoor afternoon together. When you're through, wash the dishes together, then settle down to a craft project, or a great old movie, or manicures and pedicures for everyone, or a special time of prayer. Before you know it, you might find yourselves pulling the tea things out once again—for yet another warm teatime.

Teatime Treats

Menu Suggestions:

JAM TEA
IRISH OATMEAL SCONES
"NOT REALLY FROM DEVONSHIRE CREAM"
SHORTBREAD COOKIES

JAM TEA

This is the kind of sweet specialty we all enjoyed as children. Why not share it with your friends?

> 1 pot hot English Breakfast tea
> 1 teaspoon jam per cup of tea—try raspberry,
>   strawberry, apricot, or even mint
> sugar to taste
> whipped cream (optional)

Place 1 teaspoon jam in the bottom of a cup. Pour the hot tea over the jam and stir. Add sugar and top with whipped cream if desired.

IRISH OATMEAL SCONES

Scones don't have to look like biscuits or wedges. This easy variation came from a farmhouse in Ireland. Enjoy with sweet jam and imitation clotted cream. This recipe will make 12-muffin shaped scones.

nonstick cooking spray
¾ cup milk or cream
1 large egg
3-4 tablespoons light brown sugar
1 teaspoon vanilla

2 ¼ cups all-purpose flour
1 cup old-fashioned rolled oats
1 tablespoon double-acting baking powder
½ teaspoon baking soda
½ teaspoon salt
¾ stick (6 tablespoons) cold, unsalted butter,
    cut into small pieces
½ cup dried currants (or raisins)

Spray a 12-cup muffin pan with nonstick spray and set
aside. In a bowl, whisk together milk, egg, brown sugar,
and vanilla. In another bowl, stir together dry ingredients.
Use a pastry blender or two knives to cut butter into dry
ingredients until mixture resembles coarse meal. Stir in the
currants and the milk mixture until mixture just forms a
sticky dough. Drop by ⅓-cup measures into prepared
muffin cups and bake in the middle of a preheated 400°
oven for 15-18 minutes, or until golden.

"NOT REALLY FROM DEVONSHIRE" CREAM

*It's almost impossible to find real English clotted cream here in
the United States. This delicious dairy mixture makes an accept-
able substitute. Real comfort food!*

½ pint whipping cream
1 tablespoon sour cream
3 tablespoons confectioners' sugar

Chill bowl and beaters, then whip all
ingredients together in a bowl. Keep
refrigerated. Serve with scones.

Crafter's Corner
AN EASY, FLEECY TEA COZY

A tea cozy is really a warm little sweater or jacket for your teapot. It helps keep the tea warm while you linger over your cups of tea. Here's a very quick and very easy way to put together a tea cozy out of microfleece. It will look like a warm little ski hat with the handle and spout sticking through little slits in the side—so they don't get too warm to handle.

To make it, you'll need about ½ yard of the fleece, plus standard sewing supplies—a tape measure, scissors, pins, sewing machine or needle and thread, and iron. In addition, you'll need a flat ruler, a pen or pencil, and a medium-sized rubber band.

To make the simplest kind of cozy, cut a rectangle of fleece in the following dimensions: (1) Height = height from table to top of teapot lid, measured with a tape measure loosely following the curves of the pot, plus 3 ½ inches; (2) Width = the circumference of the pot at the widest point, not counting the handle and spout—you might have to estimate in some places—plus 1 inch.

Point the short edges of the rectangle together with right sides facing and sew with a ½-inch seam. Press seam flat. Press under ½ inch along one edge and stitch ¼ inch from fold to make a bottom hem. You should now have a tall fleece tube. Lay it flat with the seam right down the middle, but don't turn it right side out yet.

Set your teapot on a table or shelf where it is at your eye level. Stand the fleece tube next to it and mark a vertical slit on each side where the spout and handle should come out. With scissors, carefully cut these slits in each side.

To make the top fringe, use a pencil to draw a line around the top of the tube, about 2 ½ inches from the edge. Make a series of cuts from the top edge down to this line. The cuts should be about ½ inch apart but don't have to be exact—you can make them freehand. Now it is ready to be turned right side out.

Place the cozy over the top of the pot and pull the handle and spout through the side openings. With your hands, gather together the top edge above the lid and secure with a rubber band. Adjust the gathers as necessary. Then cover the rubber band with an 18-inch strip of fleece, preferably cut from the finished (selvage) edge of the fabric. Just tie it in a jaunty bow, and your warm, fuzzy tea cozy is ready to warm your teapot.

A "Good for You!" Tea

When we reach out to others, they reach out to us.
It's a two-way street,
a street practically lined with balloons and streamers in
celebration of the unique bonds of friendship.
—LUCI SWINDOLL

"Hooray for you!" "Good work!" "I'm so happy you're happy!" Who doesn't love to hear those kinds of words? There's so much we can accomplish in life if we know someone is cheering us on. And that's part of what friends are for. Applauding each other's accomplishments and recognizing each other's milestones is simply something that friends do. We need our friends to help us celebrate just as surely as we need friends to help us navigate hard times.

Think back on the important occasions of your life—landmark birthdays, religious ceremonies, graduations, your wedding, the arrival of your children. Can you remember those days without also remembering the faces of special friends who shared them with you? I can't!

And don't you feel an important bond with those friends who allowed you to share their own times of joy and celebration? That's especially true for me. My memories of my friends are inescapably tied in with my memories of shared birthdays and anniversaries and weddings and other celebrations.

All this is good reason to strengthen your connection with current friends by gathering together to celebrate the good things that happen in your lives. Has one of your friends landed a new job, earned a diploma, or acquired a new grandbaby? Is someone you care about approaching a special anniversary? Has something wonderful happened—like a new house or twenty-pound weight loss—that calls for shared rejoicing? You can beautifully celebrate both the occasion and your wonderful friendships by inviting a group of friends to a "good for you!" tea. It's a warm, colorful hurrah that can't help but draw you all closer together.

A tea of this sort adapts beautifully for traditional celebrations—it'll give a different twist to wedding or baby showers, a birthday, or a commemorative holiday such as Mother's Day. And keep in mind that the "good for you" doesn't have to be just for one person! This special teatime can easily become a "good for us" party that celebrates a group accomplishment—or even just your friendship itself.

When you invite guests to the tea, make sure you inform them of the party's purpose—and whether gifts would be expected. Then, after the party starts, plan on a little bit of pomp and ceremony. Consider a little testimonial, a speech from the guest of honor, or a toast with teacups. The point is to do whatever you can think of to make a "big deal" out of the celebration, to make it feel memorable to the one you are celebrating. Honor her with a corsage in colors to match your tea. Present her with gifts, if appropriate, or, for a touch of whimsy, a laurel wreath, or "Queen for a Day" crown.

Be sure and take lots of photographs of the occasion and plan to put them in an album or scrapbook for the honoree. And don't forget to gather everyone for a group shot—a beautiful visual record of friends who care enough to celebrate together.

Teatime Treats

Menu Suggestions:

MANGO TEA
CELEBRATION SANDWICHES
"EASY AS CAKE" CONFETTI COOKIES
RAINBOW SHERBET
BABY CARROTS AND CELERY STICKS

CELEBRATION SANDWICHES

These colorful sandwiches will really tingle your taste buds and delight your eye.

> 2 6-ounce cans water-packed tuna, drained
> 2 tablespoons mayonnaise
> 4 teaspoons finely diced green bell pepper
> 4 teaspoons finely diced red bell pepper
> 2 tablespoons red onion, finely diced
> ½ teaspoon chopped, fresh parsley
> 1 teaspoon rice wine vinegar
> ½ teaspoon lemon juice
> 7 drops hot pepper sauce
> salt and white pepper to taste
> 1 loaf fine-textured white or wheat bread
>   unsalted butter, softened

Combine all ingredients but bread and butter and mix
well. Refrigerate at least one hour. Spread each slice of
bread with softened butter. Spread half the slices with tuna
mixture, then top with remaining slices. With a serrated
knife, cut off crusts and cut sandwiches into three or four
fingers. Wrap tightly in plastic wrap or cover with a damp
tea towel until ready to serve.

"EASY AS CAKE" CONFETTI COOKIES

These colorful cookies look very cheerful when arranged on a glass plate with a colored doily. If you prefer, you can add nuts instead of the chocolate chips—or omit the coconut and chips entirely. This recipe makes 4 to 5 dozen cookies.

    nonstick cooking spray
    1 8-ounce package cream cheese, room temperature
    2 eggs
    1 box confetti cake mix
    ½ cup coconut
    ½ cup white chocolate chips

Preheat oven to 350°. Lightly grease cookie sheets with cooking spray. In a bowl, beat cream cheese and egg together with an electric mixer. Add cake mix, coconut, and white chocolate chips, and mix well. Drop by teaspoonfuls onto cookie sheet. (Dough will be sticky. If you wish, you can chill for several hours to make it easier to handle.) With wet fingers, press down cookies a little and smooth edges. Bake for 8-10 minutes, until edges brown. Allow to cool 1 minute on cookie sheet, then remove to wire racks to cool completely.

Crafter's Corner
A CELEBRATION TABLE

If you own a glass-topped dining table, you can add a refreshing twist to your celebration table with just a little paint. Simply clean the underside of your table with commercial glass cleaner and use acrylic craft paints to dot colorful confetti directly on the glass.

If you like, you could even get very creative and paint festive garlands around the table's edge or words of congratulations to the guest of honor—just remember to paint backward so the words will read correctly from the top. This technique adapts very easily to any kind of glass— from the inside of the storm door to the coffee tables in the living room or even your glass plates. (Just be sure to paint on the undersides so that the paint doesn't interfere with the food.) When you're through with the party, you'll find the paint comes off easily with a spritz of glass cleaner and some paper towels.

A "Tea Potluck" for Your Larger Circle of Friends

*Our friends are the continuous threads
that help hold our lives together.*
—SARAH BAN BREATHNACH

Warm, wonderful, intimate teas don't have to be just for two or three—or even six or seven—special friends. With a little planning and care, you can extend that delicious sense of closeness and empathy to a much larger group— your office, the women in your church, a club meeting, a conference, or some other event. Hosting such a tea could even be a fun project for your smaller group of friends. You could get together and plan an elegant tea for your larger circle of acquaintances.

And here's a fun idea: Why not lighten the load a little by holding a tea "potluck"? It's not strictly traditional, but it can easily fit the warm, embracing spirit of the tea party—plus it's a great way to widen your circle of friends, expand your recipe files, and enjoy a wonderful time.

Here's how it works. You and your planning partners do the planning and invite the guests. You provide the beautiful room, the program, and, of course, the tea. But you invite each guest to bring a delectable teatime treat to share. If you ask them to bring the recipes as well, you can compile them into a booklet later and make them available to everyone who attended.

For a large group, it usually works best to assign each guest to a specific table—use place cards to mark the places. Each table should have a hostess whose responsibility is to decorate the table, serve the tea, and make sure each guest is happy.

As with any potluck, part of the fun of this party will be simply sampling the goodies and enjoying the fellowship, but some form of entertainment would add to the fun. Choose entertainment appropriate to the teatime setting and to your particular gathering. A string quartet, a pianist, a harpist, or a cellist would be lovely, but an

inspirational talk or a dramatic reading might also serve. You don't necessarily have to spend a lot of money for someone to perform. A musical group from a local high school or college or a local amateur ensemble might be happy to play for little or nothing. Or members of your group might like to show-case their talents—an afternoon's entertainment in the classic Victorian sense.

Teatime Treats

Menu Suggestions:

TEA CONCENTRATE FOR A CROWD
ORANGE ALMOND STICKY ROLLS
CRESCENT COOKIES
ORANGE WEDGES

TEA CONCENTRATE FOR A CROWD

You can brew this concentrate up to two hours ahead and still serve hot, perfectly brewed tea to your guests. This recipe makes about fifty cups of tea, but you can make more or less concentrate according to your needs. Just remember: To make tea in quantity, don't brew longer—use more tea!

   1½ cups loose tea or 16 family–sized tea bags
   2½ quarts boiling water

Pour boiling water over tea in a large nonmetallic container such as an earthenware crock. Let steep for five minutes, then strain the tea leaves or remove the tea bags. Store concentrate at room temperature until needed. To serve, use about two tablespoons of concentrate per five-ounce cup— or about three parts of water to every part concentrate. Simply place the desired amount of the concentrate in a cup or pot and then add the hot water.

   Note: This concentrate also makes delicious iced tea. Add four tablespoons to an eight-ounce glass of water, then add ice.

ORANGE ALMOND STICKY ROLLS

These are the very definition of easy and delicious!

    1 8-ounce package refrigerated crescent dinner rolls
    1 tablespoon melted butter
    ⅓ cup brown sugar
    ¼ cup teaspoon ground cinnamon
    1 tablespoon grated orange peel
    ¼ cup finely slivered almonds, plus more to sprinkle
    ⅔ cup sifted confectioners' sugar
    2 tablespoons frozen orange juice concentrate
    2 teaspoons water
    ⅛ teaspoon almond extract

Heat oven to 375°. Lightly grease a miniature muffin pan. On a lightly floured surface, unroll the crescent-roll dough and press the perforations to seal the dough into one large rectangle. Brush with melted butter. In a small bowl, combine sugar, cinnamon, orange peel, and ¼ cup finely slivered almonds. Sprinkle evenly over the dough. Starting at one long side, roll up the dough jellyroll fashion. Place on a cutting board with seam down and cut into 1-inch slices. Place each slice with cut side down into a lightly greased miniature muffin pan. Bake for 11-13 minutes or until golden. While the rolls are baking, combine powdered sugar and orange juice concentrate. Add water and extract and stir until smooth. When rolls are done, remove them from the pans immediately and drizzle with orange glaze. Sprinkle with remaining almonds.

SALT DOUGH RECIPE FOR PLACE CARDS

These easy-to-make place cards add a personal touch to your tea table and are a great souvenir for your friends to take home. They will be a fond remembrance of what a wonderful time your guests shared with treasured friends.

> 2 cups flour
> 1 cup salt
> ½ cup to 1 cup water

Mix flour and salt. Add water a tablespoon at a time until mixture forms a kneadable dough. Turn out onto a lightly floured surface and knead for about ten minutes. Roll out to a ⅜-inch thickness. Use cookie cutters to cut dough into desired shapes—a teapot would be especially cute for place cards. In addition, for each two place cards, cut a 2 by 4-inch rectangle out of the rolled dough. Cut the rectangle from corner to corner to make two long triangles. These will be the props that hold the place cards upright. Place the cutouts on a cookie sheet and bake in a very slow oven (150° to 200°) until completely hard—at least several hours. When the dough has cooled completely, paint the place cards with acrylic paint and then paint the guest's name on top. Let paint dry, then spray front and back with several layers of polyurethane varnish. Spray the triangular cutouts as well. When all is dry, use a hot-glue gun to attach the two-inch edge of the triangle to the bottom of the place cards.

Note: If you want the place cards to lean back slightly, experiment with the shape of the prop. If you trim the 2-inch edge at a little more of an angle, the place card will lean back just a little bit, showing off the name and graciously inviting your friends to sit down and take tea.

An Herbal Teatime Reunion

When twilight drops her curtain down
And pins it with a star;
Remember that you have a friend
Though she may wander far.

—LUCY MAUD MONTGOMERY
Anne of Green Gables

"Keep in touch!"
We've all said it at one time or another to friends who were moving away from us in one way or another—to another city, to another job, or to another era of life. We've heard it, too, from beloved friends gathered to tell us goodbye. Most people realize instinctively that friendships are precious investments, well worth the time and trouble of maintaining even when time and distance and circumstance alter the relationship.

"Keeping in touch" isn't always easy, though. Cards, letters, phone calls, and e-mails can all help us maintain contact with our dear friends from other times in our lives, but eventually we find ourselves longing to get together just one more time—to share the common memories that bind us together and the divergent ones that

41

have changed us since those together days.

That, of course, is the reason for reunions. They are times when we pay tribute to the friendships that have made us what we are, even as we nurture and renew the bonds that make keeping in touch worthwhile. The memories we savor together linger and haunt us like the piquant aromas of herbs from the garden and the sweetness of summer flowers. How fitting to organize a reunion of old friends around a theme of herbs and flowers—especially rosemary, the herb that signifies remembrance.

This can be a lovely tea to hold outdoors on a bright blue summer day or inside on a crisp fall day. If you are a gardener or have access to a garden, this tea will be especially easy to plan and prepare for, but lacking such a resource, you can find most of what you need at a good florist, an herb farm, a nursery, or even a supermarket.

You don't really need to plan activities. It's very unlikely you'll be at a loss for words with old and dear friends. But a little advance planning can make it even more fun for your guests to reminisce and catch up with each other's lives. Have plenty of photos on hand, plus yearbooks, old letters, and other memorabilia. And don't forget a stereo that plays the "good old songs," whether on vinyl, tape, or CD!

An especially fun idea for a reunion tea is to prepare for each guest a remembrance album, or if you prefer, an update album. Call or write ahead of time to collect information and photos from the time you were together as well as the current time. Then use these resources with your computer or a copy machine to design a page or section for each friend in attendance—and be sure to include her address, phone number, and e-mail address if she has one. Copy a set of all the personal pages for each guest, bind them together into a booklet or scrapbook with a pretty cover, and have them on hand when everyone arrives. They'll be great conversation starters and wonderful mementos of a lovely time of warm herbal tea, warm muffins, and even warmer friendships.

Teatime Treats

Menu Suggestions:

ROSEMARY CHEDDAR MUFFINS
TORTILLA CHIPS WITH SALSA
LEMON-BLUEBERRY SOUR CREAM CAKE WITH PANSIES
SUGARED GRAPES

ROSEMARY CHEDDAR MUFFINS

A savory and delicious twist on a traditional muffin. If you like these, try substituting other herbs such as basil, thyme, or a fines herbes mixture for the rosemary.

2 cups unsifted all-purpose flour
2 tablespoons baking powder
½ teaspoon salt
2 eggs
1 tablespoon honey
1 cup milk
2 tablespoons fresh
   rosemary, chopped
⅛ teaspoon cayenne or dried mustard
½ cup sharp cheddar, finely shredded

Heat oven to 400°. Grease regular-sized muffin tins with oil or cooking spray or line with paper liners. Sift the dry ingredients together and stir in the cheese and rosemary. In another bowl, beat the eggs, then add the oil, honey, and milk. Combine the dry and liquid ingredients and mix just until blended. Pour batter into muffin cups, sprinkle with a little extra cheese, and bake for 25 minutes or until done. Let cool slightly before removing from pan.

Lemon-Blueberry Sour Cream Cake with Pansies

Luscious and lemony and decked with purple pansies to match the purple berries inside, this cake will be a star on your tea table. It will serve at least 16 people and probably more.

3 cups flour
¼ teaspoon baking soda
½ teaspoon salt
1 cup butter, softened
2 tablespoons lemon juice or 2 teaspoons lemon extract
grated peel of two lemons
3 cups sugar
6 eggs
1 cup sour cream
2 cups frozen blueberries

Glaze:
2 cups confectioners' sugar
½ cup fresh lemon juice
pansies in assorted colors (grown without pesticide)
   to garnish

Preheat oven to 350°. Grease and flour a large tube pan. In a medium bowl, sift flour, soda, and salt. Cream the butter in a large mixing bowl; add lemon peel and lemon juice, gradually adding sugar. Beat two minutes. Beat in eggs two at a time, mixing thoroughly after each addition and two to three minutes after all the eggs have been added. Add half the flour and mix on lowest speed until blended. Add all the sour cream, the rest of the flour, and mix until smooth. Fold in blueberries. Pour batter into prepared pan, smooth the top, and bake for 60-80 minutes. Cool 20 minutes in the pan, then turn onto a cooling rack. After cake is completely cool, mix confectioners' sugar and lemon juice to form a smooth glaze. Drizzle over top of cake, then decorate edges and top of cake with pansies.

A WREATH FOR REMEMBRANCE

"As for Rosemary," wrote Sir Thomas More centuries ago, "I lette it runne all over my garden walls, not onlie because my bees love it, but because it is the herb sacred to remembrance and to friendship."

This fragrant herb's reminiscent qualities plus its lacy beauty make it a perfect material for concocting dainty wreaths to hang over the back of each guest's chair for a fragrant welcome. Then invite your guests to take them home and hang them to dry as a fitting remembrance of your time together.

To make miniature heart-shaped wreaths, you will need: heavy-gauge wire and wire cutters; a roll of silver florist's wire; scissors; a collection of rosemary branches cut into short sprays; some lengths of satin ribbon in colors purple, gold, ivory, or green; a glue gun; and dried or silk pansies to decorate.

Begin your wreath by twisting a length of wire into a six-inch circle. Then, by pinching it at the base and the top, form it into a heart shape. Cut short sprays of rosemary. Beginning at the "dip" at the top of the heart and working around toward the point, wire the sprays to the heart with the florist's wire. Adjust the rosemary needles as you go to conceal the wire—and overlap the base of each new spray with the end of the previous one. Tie the ribbon to the top to conceal the ends of the first stems. Hot-glue a couple of pansy blossoms onto the center of the ribbon.

SOMETHING TO THINK ABOUT—A FRIEND YOU ALREADY HAVE

Can a friend be a sister? Or a mother or daughter? What about a colleague or a teacher or the woman who grooms your dog? What about a husband?

One of the most beautiful things about friendship is that it can transcend categories and roles. In fact, you never know when a person wearing one name tag in your life—grandma, niece, neighbor, child's teacher, pastor's wife, casual acquaintance—might step over the labels and sign up as a treasured friend of the heart.

There is a mystery to the ways of friendship. After all, finding a friend is like discovering a treasure. Finding a friend in someone you already love is like finding a treasure in the rafters of your own attic—one of life's most joyful surprises!